COOL CAREERS
WITHOUT COLLEGE
FOR PEOPLE WHO LOVE
GAMING

COOL CAREERS
WITHOUT COLLEGE
FOR PEOPLE WHO LOVE
GAMING

ADAM FURGANG

ROSEN
PUBLISHING®

New York

*For my sons, Ben and Caleb—the two best gamers I know,
and my favorite gaming partners.*

Published in 2017 by The Rosen Publishing Group, Inc.
29 East 21st Street, New York, NY 10010

Copyright © 2017 by The Rosen Publishing Group, Inc.

First Edition

Library of Congress Cataloging-in-Publication Data

Names: Furgang, Adam, author.
Title: Cool careers without college for people who love gaming / Adam Furgang.
Description: First edition. | New York : Rosen Publishing, [2017] | Series:
  Cool careers without college | Includes bibliographical references and
  index.
Identifiers: LCCN 2016017846 | ISBN 9781508172826 (library bound)
Subjects: LCSH: Video games—Design—Juvenile literature. | Video
  gamers—Juvenile literature. | Computer programming—Vocational
  guidance—Juvenile literature.
Classification: LCC GV1469.3 .F865 2017 | DDC 794.8—dc23
LC record available at https://lccn.loc.gov/2016017846

Manufactured in Malaysia

CONTENTS

INTRODUCTION

Video games are interactive, story-based scenarios or puzzles in which players manipulate dynamic action on a computer monitor or a television screen. From its early popularity back in the 1970s with coin arcade games like *Pac-Man*, to the contemporary high-definition immersive home console games like *Destiny*, *Fallout 4, and Star Wars Battlefront*, the video game industry has seen a lot of change and considerable growth.

Today three gaming systems dominate the home console market: the Sony Playstation 4, Microsoft Xbox One, and the Nintendo Wii U. Overall revenue in the video game industry for 2015 was over $91 billion and will continue to grow. In 2015, mobile games used on smart phones and computer tablets overtook game sales on console-based game sales.

The video game industry has become popular around the world, with many large expos and conferences for professionals and enthusiasts. There, industry professionals mingle with amateur players and competive eSport stars, as well as meet the creators, designers, and actors who make games compelling.

Alongside the video game industry is the traditional hobby gaming industry. This includes board games, collectible games, card and dice games, collectable miniatures, and roleplaying games. Retail sales for traditional hobby gaming rose to $880 million as of 2014. Playing games both video and traditional are extremely popular pastimes globally.

Interactive video games and traditional hobby gaming are certainly fun entertainment for people of all ages, but they are also a very big business that continues to grow and evolve year after year. If you already love gaming, then a career somewhere in the gaming industry might be what you are interested in pursuing. But what is the next logical step? How can a person who loves games find their way into an increasingly multifaceted, complex, and technical industry? And as college tuition continues to rise, is it possible to find a job in the gaming industry without a college education?

America's student-loan debt now grows $2,726 every second, totaling over $1 trillion in 2016. Two-thirds of college and university students graduating today will carry some amount of student debt. The federal debt is almost at $17 trillion and student loans account for 6 percent of that. Seventeen percent of borrowers are behind on their student loan payments, and only 27 percent of college graduates have a job related to their field of study in college.

Traditional college majors often do not provide the education needed to go into the gaming industry. With the rising cost of education and the daunting prospect of taking on heavy student loans, a college education is becoming out of reach for many students.

All is not lost, however. Within the gaming industry, both traditional and video games, there are many career paths you can follow without having to go to college first. Programming, writing, art, design, music, voice acting, game design, gaming start-ups, and sales and marketing are just some of the areas you may be interested in related to gaming. Because entry-level positions after college may not lead you exactly where you want to be, you will need persistence, practice, grit, and determination to move forward; self-educate, and immerse yourself in the area of gaming you wish to have a career in. In the long run, hard work and persistence will pay off—and it can be done even without a college education. This book provides information about careers in different aspects of the gaming industry, with helpful resources for learning more about each.

CHAPTER 1

REACHING THE GAMING CUSTOMER

If you are reading this resource, odds are that you are already a gamer—video or traditional—and you likely also have a desire to move into some creative or entrepreneurial aspect of the gaming industry. Perhaps you're thinking of doing it without a college education. While many of the more glamorous gaming jobs—such as programmer, designer, and artist—are accessible, the fastest and easiest way to get yourself through the door and start earning money in the gaming industry is in retail.

WORKING AT A STORE

Big gaming companies as well as retail outlets like GameStop require sales

The most accessible place for a gamer to work is at a video game retailer. This can help keep you up to date on the latest games and trends. It also allows game enthusiatists to interface with gamers and industry professionals in a new way, outside of playing the games.

people, store clerks, and managers to help sell games to consumers. Anywhere games are sold, even used games, can be a great place to start getting experience. No college degree is required. In fact, some stores may even hire you before you are eighteen years old. Be sure to check your local stores before applying.

Video game stores, toy stores, bookstores, and electronics stores all sell video and traditional games. If you are already knowledgeable about games, this can help you land a job in a store. Many entry-level positions are available for selling games to the public. Advancing your career can come of the following responsibilities:

- Handling store promotions
- Setting up advertising displays
- Becoming a store manager
- Helping to open a new store

Working in gaming retail will allow you to communicate with gamers, get exposure to game companies, and handle game promotions, contests, and new product launches. All are valuable assets that provide experience that looks good on a résumé, even if your ultimate goal is not in sales, but another aspect of game creation.

You could also consider another closely related retail job. For example, a mobile phone company, computer retail store, or electronics store will hire someone who loves games and

Working directly for a gaming company can provide opportunities to test and demonstrate new products before they are released to the public. For example, this is a tester of a virtual reality (VR) headset. These are becoming more prevelant in the marketplace.

Attending large gaming conventions is a great way to network, meet people in the industry, and learn about new products. Often, the newest, best and brightest are being represented to consumers and retail specialists alike. It's also a chance to meet the stars associated with a gaming franchise.

also has experience with the latest technologies. Many customers who shop in larger chain stores need help finding what they need. A strong knowledge of the various gaming systems can land you a job in the gaming department, where you can answer questions and gain experience.

A few years working in retail while studying at home and building skills directly related to a specific aspect of the gaming industry like programming or game design is a great way to make money and stay current on all aspects of what is being created and sold in the industry while you move toward a greater goal.

WORKING AT A CORPORATION

In addition to selling to the public, there are also sales

positions available in large game companies where games are sold to distributors and retailers. Game companies also have many administrative positions that include duties such as:

- Arranging product launches
- Distributing promotional material
- Facilitating customer service with stores as well as consumers
- Organizing conventions and other industry events

Sales jobs at these companies are often entry-level positions, with no prior experience necessary. And if you have already worked at a small gaming store your experience might help you get a better sales position that does require some prior experience.

These various jobs will provide a steady stream of income as you explore other gaming interests and hone your skills as a writer, artist, musician, programmer, or entrepreneur for future work in the game industry.

PREPARING YOURSELF

High school students can begin a sales career working at local stores and interacting with the public and store managers to gain sales experience. Some companies may not hire you until you are eighteen. If you want a part-time job before

TECH SUPPORT AND CUSTOMER SUPPORT

Video game companies offer online and telephone support to users who need help with their consoles and video games. Someone who is very knowledgeable about video games can do well in this field. These positions often require a minimum of a high school diploma as well as some level of familiarity with basic programs such as Windows operating systems and Microsoft Word.

If you have already worked in retail, your experience communicating with customers can be looked on as a valuable skill. Familiarity with current games and gaming systems, and their inner menus, settings, and technical details, will all come in handy when applying for a job like this. Search online for jobs in gaming technical support to see what is available.

you are eighteen, an internship is something to consider. An internship is a program, often related to a school course, in which you work at a company. Many internships offer school credit but little or no pay. They offer valuable experience in the industry you aspire to work in. Check local gaming companies to see if they have internship programs available and what is required. Your school guidance department may also be able to connect you with internship opportunities or the possibility of getting school credit.

Staying current on video and board games will help you understand the merchandise and industry. For many gamers, there is a spot between a casual consumer and working professional where you can be more involved than the average at-home gamer while still not being employed in the industry. Playing in industry-sanctioned weekly gaming groups at local gaming stores or larger convention tournaments are both good ways to keep current and involved, even if you have not gotten into the industry yet.

FUTURE PROSPECTS

With the increase in online download sales for digital content, careers in retail video gaming sales at brick and mortar stores may experience slower growth than in the past. People increasingly tend to buy their games online as digital downloads. Career growth at video game companies may be more promising because of the overall growth of the industry in general. Traditional board games and role-playing games (RPGs) are still mostly sold in boxes and as physical books, so retail jobs selling these games will not be going away any time soon.

FOR MORE INFORMATION

BOOKS

Donovan, Tristan. *Replay: The History of Video Games.* East Sussex, England: Yellow Ant, 2010.
Donovan provides a comprehensive history of video games from the 1980s to today, with over 140 interviews with game designers and developers.

Funk, Joe. *Cool Careers in Interactive Entertainment: Hot Jobs in Video Games.* New York, NY: Scholastic, 2010.
Funk offers readers an introduction to the world of video game creation by providing profiles of professionals in a wide range of jobs in the video game field.

Nichols, Randy. *The Video Game Business.* London, England: British Film Institute, 2014.
Nichols gives a historical, economic, and cultural overview of the video game industry, including changes in gaming audiences and the labor needed to produce games.

ORGANIZATIONS

Entertainment Merchants Association
16530 Ventura Boulevard, Suite 400

Encino, CA 91436-4551

(818) 385-1500

Website: http://www.entmerch.org

The EMA is a nonprofit organization dedicated to merchants who sell multimedia entertainment, including computer and console video games.

The Game Manufacturers Association

240 N. Fifth Street, Suite 340

Columbus, OH 43215

(614) 255-4499

Website: http://gama.org

GAMA is a nonprofit organization dedicated to the tabletop game industry. It provides educational programs to promote tabletop entertainment.

PERIODICALS

Game Trade

10150 York Road, Suite 300

Hunt Valley, MD 21030

(443) 318-8232

Website: http://www.gametrademagazine.com

This monthly magazine provides product information for game and hobby supplies.

WEBSITES

Due to the changing nature of internet links, Rosen Publishing has developed an online list of websites related to the subject of this book. This site is updated regularly. Please use this link to access the list:

http://www.rosenlinks.com/CCWC/game

CHAPTER 2

GET YOUR GAME ON

Professional gaming, or eSports, is fast becoming a full-fledged competitive spectator sport in its own right. ESport events also have live video game competitions with fans that fill large stadiums, just like traditional physical sports. ESports revenue for 2015 in North America was $134 million.

Established video games like *League of Legends and DotA 2* ("*DotA*" stands for *Defense of the Ancients*) have large fan bases that often watch and sometimes participate in live tournaments. A 2015 *League of Legends* regional championship match at Madison Square Garden in New York City had eleven thousand fans in attendance. In 2015, more than 134 million viewers watched eSports around the world. *DotA*

Members of the competitive gaming team, Newbee, pose on the stage of the International DOTA 2 Championships in Seattle Washington in 2014. These events draw huge crowds to the audience as the games are shown in real time.

2 holds an annual eSports championship tournament called The International. In 2015, The International was held in the KeyArena Center in Seattle, Washington. The prize pool was over $18 million, the biggest prize pool in eSports history at the time. The winning team, Evil Geniuses, won $6,634,660, and each player in the team received over $1.3 million.

In 2013, the United States government recognized international video game players travellinng to the United States to compete in a *League of Legends* tournament as professional athletes for the very first time. This made it easier for special visas to be issued to players visiting the United States for professional play. According to a *GameSpot* magazine interview with Nick Allen, a Riot Games eSports manager, "This is groundbreaking for eSports; now we can start looking at international players when they come over. It's a much easier process because they're actually recognized by the government." ESports is now a big business with many opportunities to find work.

Some of the skills needed to make eSports a career include:

- Exceptional gaming skills
- Good communication skills with teammates
- Attention to detail when signing up for competitions
- Professional behavior at competitive events
- Professional behavior with sponsors or potential sponsors

GAME TESTING

Before companies can release video games for sale, they need to be thoroughly tested for bugs and glitches so that they work correctly upon release. The age range of game testers starts with very young children who test kids and youth games and goes all the way up to people getting paid for a living to test games. Younger testers often get their name listed in the credits of the game.

Game testing is not just for video games, either. In 2012, the gaming company Wizards of the Coast released an early beta version of the current fifth iteration of the classic role-playing game *Dungeons & Dragons* to the general public for play testing. Local *Dungeons & Dragons* gaming groups were able to test play and provide feedback directly to Wizards of the Coast to help shape the fifth edition of *Dungeons & Dragons*. The fifth edition starter set was released for sale on July 15, 2014. Even if you only volunteer to test play a game, this valuable experience can still be listed on a résumé when applying for a professional game testing job.

MAKING MONEY

Making money as a professional gamer is not easy, but it can be done, and it does not require a college education. You need to be a fantastic gamer, and not just at any game, either. Some of the more popular games for professional play are: *League of Legends*, *Counter-Strike: Global Offensive*, *DotA 2*, *Hearthstone*, *Smite*, *World of Warcraft*, *Heroes of the Storm*, and *Super Smash Bros*. Getting great at one of these games will be a must if you are going to pursue professional gaming as a career. Although many people may say it is a long shot, there are people already doing this for a living. The attention the growing popularity is giving the emerging entertainment is only getting bigger. The most successful professionals can make six figure incomes from their winnings alone, not including salaries from teams or sponsors.

Members of a professional gaming team must play and work well together to succeed in eSports.

Professional gamers often have knowledge of how computers work. This comes in handy when customizing and upgrading for speed in competition. Gamers may have a hand in or even build from scratch their ideal computer system to support rapid gameplay and multiple complex features.

Pro gamers are paid to be on teams, and often get paid by sponsors to endorse products or gaming companies, which adds to their incomes. Professional gamers can also compete alone or on small teams for prize pool money.

GAMING COMPUTERS

If you want to be a professional gamer, or even just play competitive gaming online, you will need a good gaming computer, as well as a high speed internet connection. Games played by professional gamers are not typically played on home gaming consoles such as the Xbox or Playstation. Many competitive video games are available to buy or as digital downloads for Microsoft Windows, and for Apple Mac OS X and SteamOS, Linux-based PC computers. Some companies manufacture computers specifically for avid gamers. These are called gaming computers, or gaming rigs, and have very fast CPUs (central processing units) and GPUs (graphics processing units) or video cards that will help run the games very efficiently.

PROFESSIONAL COSPLAY

Cosplay (costumed play) is a unique phenomenon in which people dress up as their favorite science fiction, fantasy, or manga characters. Cosplayers can typically be found at comic, science fiction, and gaming conventions. Most people who engage in cosplay typically dress up just for fun. Some people, though, have managed to make a living dressing up as costumed characters. Some have even earned a considerable amount of money by dressing up and turning a hobby into a profession.

Many professional cosplayers sew and create their own costumes and props from scratch. Some of the fanciest custom costumes are worn by professionals who get paid for convention appearances, game promotion, photo shoots, and modeling work. Selling signed prints at conventions or online is another way to make money at cosplay. Engaging in many social media outlets like Twitter and Instagram helps to get some cosplayers thousands of loyal fans.

These professional cosplayers are performing the *Legend of Zelda* during the World Cosplay Summit at the Tokyo International Film Festival in 2014. Many fans become involved with cosplay as a way to get involved and show their passion for a franchise while attending conventions and other gaming events.

Many professional gamers customize their own computers by buying and assembling the various components, such as a motherboard, graphics cards, cooling fans, hard drives, and RAM chips. Computers customized by gamers are typically designed for performance and require the newest components as they become available. Having a fast computer is important for competitive game play.

PREPARING YOURSELF

Don't quit your day job yet. Pro gaming is for someone who loves to play competitively and is excellent at a popular established eSports game. It's important to remember that the competition is fierce and even if you are great, there's still no promise of money or income. People interested in this field can get involved in their spare time while still earning money from more traditional sources. Download and play popular eSports games to improve your skills over time.

In addition to watching live professional games, the growing industry can also be watched online through Major League Gaming (MLG). Being a sportscaster or writer for eSports websites and online broadcast networks are other areas to consider if you love professional gaming but are not quite good enough to make money through competition.

FUTURE PROSPECTS

The industry of eSports is still in its infancy. The growth prospects in this field are above average. Even if you cannot enter the eSports field as a professional player, there are other related positions, such as managerial and organizational professionals.

FOR MORE INFORMATION

BOOKS

Romaine, Mike. *Gaming Sponsorships 101: What You Need to Know About Gaming Sponsors if You're Looking to Be Sponsored in eSports*. Seattle, WA: Amazon Digital Services, 2014.
Romaine discusses how to become sponsored as an eSports gamer, including how to apply, what sponsors expect from you, and what you should expect from any sponsors you work with.

Talmage, David. *A Gamer's Guide to Building a Gaming Computer*. Seattle, WA: Amazon Digital Services, 2016.
Talmage explores the steps for building the essential parts of a gaming computer for use in eSports.

Taylor, Lind. *An Introduction to the Growing World of E-Sports*. Seattle, WA: Amazon Digital Services, 2016.
Taylor discusses the world of electronic sports and its expansion in the business world.

Winnan, Christopher D. *An Entrepreneur's Guide to the Exploding World of eSports: Understanding the Commercial Significance of Counter-Strike, League of Legends, and DotA 2*. Benson, MD: Borderlands Press, 2016.
Winnan provides guidance and tips for becoming a commercial success in the world of eSports.

ORGANIZATIONS

International eSports Federation
5F #501, 1-1
Hangangno 3-ga
Yongsan-gu
Seoul, Korea
+82-2-715-6661
Website: http://ie-sf.com
The International eSports Federation promotes eSports
    as a sport without language, race, or cultural barriers.

Major League Gaming
East 34th Street
New York, NY 10016
Website: http://www.majorleaguegaming.com
Major League Gaming is the major sponsor and online
    broadcast source for eSports and competitive gaming
    events in the United States.

WEBSITES

Due to the changing nature of internet links, Rosen Publishing has developed an online list of websites related to the subject of this book. This site is updated regularly. Please use this link to access the list:

http://www.rosenlinks.com/CCWC/game

CHAPTER 3

WRITING THE FUTURE OF GAMES

A good foundation of any narrative is a well-written story. Having a good story for your game will make it more compelling for the player. Writing careers in the gaming industry can be as varied as the many games and platforms that exist. Writing games is just one job that a writer can have in the gaming field. A good writer can get involved in journalism and blogging related to the gaming field. Writers are also needed for game guides, game instructions, and "art of" books, as well as any text that accompanies any book produced for the gaming industry.

Full-time writing jobs at companies will be advertised online or handled through recruiting companies. However, many writers submit articles to magazines and websites on a freelance basis. This can be done by anyone,

All games, even the most complex video games, start with brainstorming and writing down ideas. Much like writing a book, the action and characters must be mapped out before design can begin.

even someone who works in another aspect of the video game industry. If you are interested in writing articles or reviews, just give it a shot by pitching editors at your favorite gaming publication. The more experience you get, the better your chances of being published become. Different companies have different rules about submitting work. Quarterly and online magazines often accept submissions. Be sure to research submission guidelines before sending in writing to a company for consideration. Keep a résumé of articles you have written, even if they have not been published. Over time, your efforts may pay off.

VIDEO GAME WRITING

Game writers have a complex job. They should have incredibly active imaginations to help conceptualize original game stories and adventures. No idea for a game should be ignored. Keep a journal of any idea that comes into your head. Some of the tasks done by a person who writes video game or board game stories include:

- Research the competition to know what other games exist in the field.
- Communicate with game designers and programmers to make sure the story concepts are able to be realistically carried out.

- Adhere to existing licensed property frameworks if working with licensed characters.
- Adhere to existing boundaries and constraints of a particular game company you may be working for, including age appropriateness and rating structures.
- Make revisions based on feedback from managers, designers, and game testers.

Whether you write games for a company or as an independent worker, the first step is to organize your plans. Because video game narratives can take many paths as players make different decisions, it is important to keep a flowchart as a guide while you write. All possible outcomes and variations must be planned in advance.

For a video game, there may be one overarching story with many side paths a player can take along the way, or there may be many different narrative outcomes depending on player choices at different points in the game. A flowchart is a guide for the way the game will be constructed and can be very helpful for game designers and artists who will need a basic framework to use as a guide. You can create a game flowchart on paper or on the computer. A flowchart may wind up looking a bit like a tree, with many branching outcomes coming off of it.

Next, create a script to guide you through the writing process. A game script will be much more specific and in-depth than a flowchart. Describe the settings and scenes with as much detail as possible. Create dialogue for each character, including the narrator. Also include the places where sound effects or music should be inserted. Notes to game designers and programmers can also be included and give descriptions of different locations, outcomes, and items. A video game script should and could be even more in-depth that a movie screenplay because you are describing many interacting elements of the game at once.

KEEP PLAYING

Game writers should play games often and pay special attention to the stories in the games being played. If you want to write specific types of games, such as only

As your game ideas grow, you can begin to craft a more complex story by writing a script with more complex characters and dialogue.

WRITING FOR THE HOBBY GAME INDUSTRY

If you are interested in writing for traditional hobby games such as role-playing and board games, you will need to stay focused on your writing and storytelling skills. The way traditional tabletop games are played is often just as important as the story or adventure being told while the game unfolds. In many games, players create their own imaginary characters using specific game rules before the game can start. Popular board games like *Star Wars Imperial Assault* or the card game *Magic the Gathering* require many game pieces, art elements, and graphically-designed elements. It may help to get the assistance of an artistic friend in visualizing the art aspects while you write the story elements.

A few popular role-playing games are *Dungeons & Dragons*, *Pathfinder*, *Star Wars*, and *Call of Cthulhu*. You may want to write new adventures for an existing game, or you can make up a new game setting that is entirely your own. Originality can help showcase your creative writing skills. Getting friends and family to test play a game you created is a great way to see your hard work in action and can help you refine your writing going forward.

role-playing board games or only console video games, then you should be playing those types of games regularly so you are familiar with what you want to write.

Games are fluid, and, unlike a film or novel that operates according to typical linear storytelling with no choices for the viewer, games often have many choices and possible outcomes a player can make. A game writer needs to be able to write out all the varied possibilities that the player might experience. Playing an existing game several times and exploring the various choices is a great way to see how the writers of a game helped to construct the story. Each outcome must be conceptualized in advance and make sense within the construct of the entire game and its mechanics.

NETWORK WITH WRITER GROUPS

Spending time with other writers can be a good way to get feedback on what you are working on, whether it's an article, game review, or even a game framework. Although writing is a solitary craft, sharing your work with others can be helpful and allow you to see your work in a critical light, which can help you to improve your writing overall. Even if you do not know other writers in the gaming field, spending time with other writers you know will keep you thinking about your craft. Share your work with gamers so they can give feedback as well. A player's opinion can be just as valuable as another writer's opinion. Getting other people's opinions can help you to find flaws in your story. It can also help you realize things you may have overlooked or that others find confusing.

COLLABORATE

Writing a novel or article tends to be a solo creative endeavor. Video game writers usually work with a team. Even if you are the only writer on a small team there will still likely be a game designer and an artist. Communication and collaboration with other team members is essential for creating a cohesive video game that plays well and makes sense. Even if you are writing a traditional board game or role-playing game, there will likely be other writers working with you, and you will need to be able to work well with others, share ideas, and easily take criticism. Many existing role-playing games have rules that will need to be adhered to. The end result of the game is what is important, and keeping an open mind and listening to other ideas, even from team members who are not writers, can be very important in the writing process.

Sharing your ideas within your gaming group is a great springboard for getting feedback for your ideas. Making games is a collaborative process, whether it is a digital game or a more traditional card or board game.

PREPARING YOURSELF

Preparing to write for the gaming industry requires a lot of reading and game playing. Keep up on gaming magazines, and read reviews and industry news. Take writing and journalism courses at school. Check online gaming communities for people looking for help in creating a home-brewed game. It will help you get credit and experience for your résumé.

FUTURE PROSPECTS

The US Bureau of Labor Statistics does not collect data on the video game industry or board game industry. However, the organization suggests that workers in this field earn more than the median annual income in the United States.

As the gaming industry grows, so will the need for support publications such as periodicals, books, stand alone novels, and game guides. Writing is a growing field in the gaming industry. In addition to writing game narratives, consider journalism and blogging as possible jobs in the gaming industry. Instruction manuals and game guides that help gamers play through games are also other areas writers can get jobs in the gaming industry.

FOR MORE INFORMATION

BOOKS

Bryant, Robert Denton, and Keith Giglio. *Slay the Dragon: Writing Great Video Games*. Studio City, CA: Michael Wiese Productions, 2015.
Bryant and Giglio provide useful advice for people who want to create interactive narratives that can be used in gaming. The book provides discussions as well as self-paced writing exercises.

Dille, Flint. *The Ultimate Guide to Video Game Writing and Design*. Los Angeles, CA: Lone Eagle Publishing, 2008.
Dille provides a solid introduction to the processes of writing and designing video games, showing how the two processes overlap each other in many ways.

Skolnick, Evan. *Video Game Storytelling: What Every Developer Needs to Know About Narrative Techniques*. New York, NY: Watson-Guptill, 2014.
Skolnick provides a how-to guide for basic storytelling for every stage of the computer game development process.

ORGANIZATIONS

International Game Developers Association (IGDA)
19 Mantua Road
Mount Royal, NJ 08061
Website: http://www.igda.org
The IGDA is a group dedicated to the needs of game
    developers, with special interest groups dedicated to
    the work of video game writers.

Writer's Guild of America, West (WGAW)
7000 West Third Street
Los Angeles, CA 90048
(323) 951-4000
Website: http://www.wga.org
The WGAW is an organization dedicated to helping
    writers in the entertainment field pursue a career,
    including video game writers.

PERIODICALS

Game Informer
724 North 1st Street, 3rd Floor
Minneapolis, MN 55401
(612) 486-6101
Website: http://www.gameinformer.com

Game Informer is a popular magazine for video game fans, and it offers many opportunities for writers to provide reviews and articles about the business.

WEBSITES

Due to the changing nature of internet links, Rosen Publishing has developed an online list of websites related to the subject of this book. This site is updated regularly. Please use this link to access the list:

http://www.rosenlinks.com/CCWC/game

CHAPTER 4

AN ARTIST'S WORLD

It's hard for a game to take off and be very popular unless it has good art to help tell the story. All games require creative illustrators with strong artistic abilities to imagine and create art for a finished product. Illustrators are often skilled in drawing and creative thinking. A game illustrator will be able to work with designers and writers in order to bring the game to life.

Game concept art is often done digitally in programs such as Photoshop or Painter. Knowledge of 3-D rendering and 3-D

The look and feel of a video game begins with an artist's ability to imagine other worlds and communicate those ideas visually. The worldbuilding stage of game design is an exciting and important part of making a game compelling.

animation is needed to help create game characters and virtual game environments. Three-dimensional modeling programs such as 3-D Studio Max, Maya, and ZBrush are some of the popular 3-D rendering programs that game artists could use to create game characters and elements.

Some of the requirements of a video game artist include:

- Making concept sketches of characters and backgrounds that will be used in a game
- Creating detailed drawings of characters or backgrounds according to an agreed-upon style
- Communicating with team members to create a look and feel consistent with the design of the project

Game artists need to be able to use traditional skills with modern computer rendering equipment. Usually there are large teams of people involved in creating a game, with each person tasked with distinct roles. All this work comes together in the final game, but there are thousands of smaller tasks involved, all of which are handed by specialists.

- Creating detailed art of characters in different positions to help with 3-D rendering
- Using computer programs employed by traditional artists or 3-D artists or animators
- Using a solid knowledge base of color theory to put together good design

The more you can communicate about your art and the game concepts you are working on, the better off you will be in the gaming art world. Visual communication is important for explaining game architecture for all members on a game team. Games like *Tomb Raider*, *The Legend of Zelda*, and *Halo* all revolve around characters. Many games take place in fantastic landscapes and futuristic worlds and are populated with imaginary species, creatures, futuristic vehicles, and fantastic-looking space ships. Artists are a very important part of creating these characters and their imaginative worlds.

IT STARTS WITH THE ART

Anyone looking to get involved in creating any type of art for any type of game should have a very strong background in drawing. The human figure, animals, and scenic backgrounds are especially important to focus on. The importance of practicing your drawing and putting together a strong portfolio cannot be overemphasized. Unless you are creating an independent game without the help of a company, a gaming company will want to see a portfolio of your work to be sure that you have the skills and experience to work for them.

Sketch artists and painters are not the only kind of artists needed in the gaming world. Traditional sculptors are also needed to create figures for traditional game pieces and playable miniatures for tabletop games. Another area a sculptor can find work in the gaming industry is in the creation of toys for games such as *Skylanders*, *Disney Infinity*, or Nintendo Amiibo figures. Some artists and sculptors are traditionally trained at art colleges, but not all of them are. Even art courses not affiliated with an undergraduate degree can help someone get started in the field.

LEARN THE TRADE

Game artists take game story ideas and help bring them to life. Concept art is the first step in the process, so everyone involved in game creation can begin to see what the game may wind up looking like. Concept art and illustrations produced by game artists will often undergo discussion and criticism. A game artist should be prepared to work with a team and generate multiple variations of the same idea, character, creature, or landscape until the design team or lead game designer agrees upon a final concept.

In addition to learning how to draw, a game artist will also need to be familiar with concepts such as perspective, color theory, depth, and various styles and mediums. Different games have different looks. A well-rounded game artist should be familiar with several painting mediums such as watercolor, colored pencils, acrylic, and oil. Different art styles such as painterly, comic book, detailed, loosely-rendered, and graphic will all be useful when determining the look of a game.

Traditional hobby games use art in books,

To hone your artistic skills, practice drawing, sketching, and painting regularly. Even if your interest is in digital work, a good command of life drawing, observational drawing, and a familiarity with a variety of styles are all useful skills for a game design artst.

"THE ART OF..."

The many coffee table style "art of" books that often accompany the release of video games can be a valuable resource for any aspiring artist. Popular hobby and video games such as the card game *Magic the Gathering*, the video game *Tomb Raider*, and the mobile game *Plants vs. Zombies* are just a few that have "art of" books.

In many of these books, the artists who conceptualize elements for the games are showcased. Many variations of concept art are exhibited for fans of the final product. Are there certain types of video games you like? Do you also want to become an artist in the industry? Picking up one of the "art of" books for a game you like is a great way to see how concept art is generated for video games.

on playing cards, and on game boards. Familiarize yourself with different games and try to imitate different styles you see. Having examples of a wide range of artistic styles will go a long way in creating a valuable portfolio and helping you become a working artist in the gaming industry.

DIGITAL ART TOOLS

Game artists should be able to sketch out concepts traditionally by hand. That skill will not likely go away for artists. Increasingly, however, many game artists work digitally with art programs such as Adobe Photoshop and Corel Painter to render artwork on the computer. Digital styluses and tablets are often used in place of traditional materials such as pencils or brushes and paints. Working digitally has lots of benefits as artists can switch mediums very easily. Finished artwork can be shared with team members and distributed quickly.

PREPARING YOURSELF

Learning to draw is probably the most important skill needed for a career in video game art. Take art courses in school, and practice drawing frequently to improve your skills. Check out YouTube for online instruction videos to learn new artistic techniques and rules through art classes online, or watch tutorials. Keeping a sketchbook and drawing people in daily life is a great way to keep your drawing skills sharp.

Check with your school to see if computer art programs are available. 3-D drawing or design programs are particularly useful. You don't need to have every program on your home computer, but free limited trials or student discounts may be available for many popular programs.

FUTURE PROSPECTS

The future of gaming art is bright, but keeping up on changing computer programs and gaming trends is important. As new technologies like virtual reality (VR) headsets are introduced into the video game industry, it is important to be able to generate art that will help communicate concepts to design teams. A command of traditonal art skills continues to be important, but in addtion, artists will need to be well versed in the various new technologies entering the market.

FOR MORE INFORMATION

BOOKS

Kennedy, Sam R. *How to Become a Video Game Artist: The Insider's Guide to Landing a Job in the Gaming World.* New York, NY: Watson-Guptill, 2013.
Kennedy provides advice and helpful tips about searching for and landing a job in the video game industry.

Melissinos, Chris, and Patrick O'Rourke. *The Art of Video Games: From Pac-Man to Mass Effect.* New York, NY: Welcome Books, 2012.
Melissinos and O'Rourke give an overview of video game art from the 1980s to the current day.

Solarski, Chris. *Drawing Basics and Video Game Art: Classic to Cutting-Edge Art Techniques for Winning Video Game Design.* New York, NY: Watson-Guptill, 2012.
Solarski provides tips and techniques for artists who love video games and are interested in pursuing their own career as a video game artist.

ORGANIZATIONS

Graphic Artists Guild
31 West 34th Street, 8th Floor
New York, NY 10001
(212) 791-3400
Website: https://www.graphicartistsguild.org
The Graphic Artists Guild helps its members build
    careers in the arts, including in the field of interactive
    and multimedia gaming.

Society of Illustrators, Artists and Designers (SIAD)
207 Regent Street, 3rd Floor
London W1B 3HH
England
SIAD is a nonprofit organization dedicated to
    promoting and protecting the work of artists and
    designers in all visual media.

WEBSITES

Due to the changing nature of internet links, Rosen Publishing has developed an online list of websites related to the subject of this book. This site is updated regularly. Please use this link to access the list:

http://www.rosenlinks.com/CCWC/game

CHAPTER 5

CONTROLLING THE LOOK WITH DESIGN

Graphic design is a broad and creative career path within the gaming industry. Books, box art, posters, video games, web games, and mobile games are examples of aspects of the field that require graphic designers. A graphic designer combines visual graphics, art, and text together in hopes of clearly communicating an idea to the viewer.

Graphic designers are problem solvers. Game designers work to find the best way to combine

Graphic designers often work within a team to communicate ideas and build gaming elements. They are the bridge between the game artists and the specialists that build the code to execute the game.

Take graphic design classes in school to get started with the basic skills you will need for working in the field. This can mean working with a selection of computer programs, but also studying color theory, layout and design concepts.

various elements together and communicate with art, color, and layout so that games are easy for players to understand. Lead graphic designers may control a whole team of designers and coordinate their work.

SKILLS TO HAVE

A graphic designer for video games will need to be creative and good at visual communication problem solving. Strong traditional drawing skills alongside computer skills are important. Designers also need knowledge of layout, typography, and color theory. A few of the typical computer programs used by graphic designers are Adobe Photoshop, Illustrator, Flash, and InDesign. A graphic designer will need to create graphics for print, web, and gaming platforms.

To learn various graphic design concepts and computer programs use the internet to search for online educational resources. Many programs used by graphic designers offer trial downloads of programs. Using a program during a trial download period is a great way to get to know the program and see if it is something you want to invest money in buying. Students can often get discounts for industry standard computer programs. Ask an art or graphic design teacher at your school to see if they can help you gain access to these programs at school.

Game industry graphic designers will often need to work with art directors and lead designers or be part of a team where each designer works on a specific part of a video game. Many games are sequels or continuations of

Making a web page or personal blog is a great first step for learning graphic design skills. Many sites allow you to build from scratch using HTML coding, or to apply various themes by other designers that you may be able to modify.

existing licensed properties. Style guides and art parameters must be used to keep new games looking similar and familiar to the player. A few tasks typically required of a graphic designer for a licensed video game are:

- Creating game backgrounds and user interfaces, often under set parameters
- Creating conceptual mockups for various game elements
- Communicating with art directors or game designers for assigned tasks
- Producing game elements from concept to completion alongside reviews and feedback

GETTING STARTED

Combining photography, art, and typography are a big part of what a graphic designer does. Before working on print or video games you can practice graphic design by working on small web pages and perhaps building a personal blog. Making choices about layout, color, and what elements go where will go a long way to helping you as your skills advance.

Even if you do not have access to a computer or the internet, you can conceptualize a simple video game in a sketchbook with colored pencils or markers. Create game characters, backgrounds, and different load screens for the

COMPANY BRANDING

One job that graphic designers do is to create company logos that communicate an idea in a simple, strong, and graphic way. A company logo helps brand a company and make people remember it when they shop for products. Some of the original video game companies such as Atari and Activision still use logos similar to their original, so consumers can quickly recognize and identify them.

One example of a simple graphic gaming company logo today is Rockstar, which simply shows an "R" and a star. Another is LucasArts, which shows a person with a head as the iris of an eye. When consumers see these logos they are visually reminded of the company's reputation and previous products.

ideas you have. Being creative, even on paper, is often the first step taken for any video game. Remember to use this simple and valuable resource. Ideas recorded on paper will help you remember your ideas and can communicate to others if you start creating a game on the computer.

If you want to make a traditional board, card, or role-playing game then using notebooks and sketchpads

FOR MORE INFORMATION

BOOKS

Inston, Jennifer. *Graphic Design: A Beginner's Guide to Mastering the Art of Graphic Design*. Seattle, WA: CreateSpace Independent Publishing Platform, 2015.
Inston presents the basics of graphic design in a descriptive and practical way, preparing the reader to gain the skills that are used in most professional design settings.

Kleon, Austin. *Steal Like an Artist: 10 Things Nobody Told You About Being Creative*. New York, NY: Workman Publishing Company, 2012.
Kleon discusses the artistic process, which involves remixing and embracing existing designs to create something new and fresh.

Sherwin, David. *Creative Workshop: 80 Challenges to Sharpen Your Design Skills*. Blue Ash, OH: HOW Books, 2010.
Sherwin provides eighty creative design challenges for readers to keep their general graphic design skills sharp and professional.

ORGANIZATIONS

American Institute of Graphic Arts (AIGA)
233 Broadway, 17th floor
New York, NY 10279
(212) 807-1990
Website: http://www.aiga.org
AIGA is the oldest and largest organization for both professional and amateur graphic artists, established in 1914 and still serving today's most cutting-edge graphic designers.

The Freelancers Union
20 Jay Street Suite 700
Brooklyn, NY 11201
(800) 856-9981
Website: http://www.freelancersunion.org
The Freelancers Union supports the work of independent contractors and freelancers, many of whom work as graphic artists. They offer benefits to members such as health care and professional development opportunities.

PERIODICALS

HOW
10151 Carver Road, Suite 200
Blue Ash, OH 45242
(513) 531-2690
Website: http://www.howdesign.com
This magazine is a useful resource and artistic
inspiration for professional graphic designers
and those just starting out. It provides news and
information about the graphic arts field and
technology tips, and it profiles professionals in
the field.

Digital Arts
101 Euston Road
London, NW1 2RA
020 7756 2800
Website: http://www.digitalartsonline.co.uk
This publication focuses on news, reviews, and
features for aa specifically digital arts audience.
The magazine provides comprehensive coverage
of graphic design, 3D work, animation and video,
as well as web and interactive design, all of which

are foundational for a good understanding of the intersection of technology and design.

WEBSITES

Due to the changing nature of internet links, Rosen Publishing has developed an online list of websites related to the subject of this book. This site is updated regularly. Please use this link to access the list:

http://www.rosenlinks.com/CCWC/game

CHAPTER 6

READY, SET, PROGRAM

All applications, games, and software programs on computers or gaming systems require specific instructions to make them run. These instructions are special computer languages, commonly called code. A programmer writes code that instructs the computer, mobile device, or game system what to do and how to run when a user plays a game. All computers and video game systems use coding languages to run games and execute user input to interact with gaming elements. The programming allows users to control the game elements by using game controllers. Many different programming languages can be used to create games for computers, video game consoles, or handheld devices.

Game programmers are essential for bringing all aspects of a game to life. They are responsible for building the game from dream to reality. Every aspect of the game, from story to visuals to play, has to be constructed out of strings of code for it to appear in a playable format for users.

Game programmers must write all of the activity that occurs during game play—from player input to nonplayer elements. Even the graphic images and 3-D elements that were created by graphic designers and artists must be controlled by a programmer's game code before the video game can function.

GAMING CODE LANGUAGES

In order to become a programmer, you will need to familiarize yourself with the various computer programming languages used to create video games. The most common in the industry today are JavaScript, Java (for Android/Google), C++ for PC and console games, and Objective-C (for iOS/Apple).

Learning a computer programming language may seem like an impossible task, but there are many online resources to help anyone, even children, learn to code. Some resources even allow you to create your own video game to run on your home computer.

Rather than starting off trying to tackle a big ambitious gaming project, it's best to

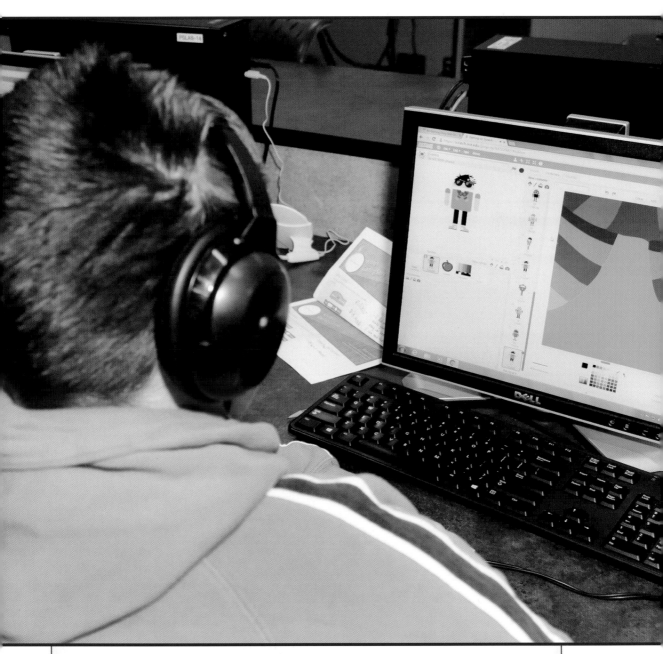

Creating a game requires a variety of tools and simulations, from coding to programs like Godot that allows designers to build and simulate the environment of the game. Some programs are free to download and use, even for amateurs, and can be used to build coding and design skills outside of formal training.

Take advantage of courses offered at your school, such as computer science or programming. They provide valuable skills for someone considering a career in the gaming field.

start small. Once you take the first steps with learning coding and creating simple actions, you will see that learning coding is not as complex as you may have once thought. One reason that coding may not be as daunting as it looks is because software exists to create video game code. This existing game creation software is referred to as a game engine. Game engines help make the job of the programmer easier.

Game engines exist as frameworks so that programmers can easily adapt them to the project they are working on. Core programming elements already exist in a game engine, and this allows game programmers to just focus on creating specific game elements unique to the game being designed. Game engines also help to manage all of the assets required to run a game and render them to the player's TV screen.

Some of the more common game engines that are used by programmers today are Unity3D, Unreal Engine, CryEngine 3, and HeroEngine. Each of these can be found online. If you are interested in learning to code, these programs are worth using.

GET DOWN TO BUSINESS

If you find that your school does not offer courses in coding, don't give up. Keep searching. Khan Academy, an online educational site, has game programming and computer language classes for free. Local community colleges may also offer classes or summer courses in programming. If possible, try to find a class that will allow you to code an entire game from start to finish. This can become an important portfolio piece when you are looking for work. Even if you don't plan on being a computer programmer, all people working on creating video games should know at least a little bit about programming. Understanding programming is important even for designers and artists, so that they know what is possible when creating a game.

The job of a computer programmer can be varied. Here are some of the tasks a programmer can expect to do on the job:

- Turn instructions from designers into codes that a computer can follow.
- Write code to make a specific game work on a designated computer platform.
- Convert the code of a game so that it works across gaming platforms. (For example, convert a game coded

for Microsoft Xbox to work on a Sony Playstation or Nintendo system.)

- Code games into an app for mobile devices.
- Correct glitches that occur in new or existing designs.

PREPARING YOURSELF

If your school offers any computer or programming courses, take them. Even if gaming is not part of the curriculum, join an online course or watch tutorials on the internet. When you are ready to apply for jobs as a programmer, familiarize yourself with questions that interviewers may ask by researching the topic. Programmers are often asked more difficult, problem-solving questions in an interview. It's also likely that a prospective employer will give you a coding test as part of the interview.

FUTURE PROSPECTS

According to the US Bureau of Labor Statistics, the outlook for computer programmers is has slightly declined. The job can be done from anywhere in the world, so companies sometimes look to hire programmers from countries where wages are lower. The salary of a computer programmer in North America is higher than the median salary for other jobs.

FOR MORE INFORMATION

BOOKS

Aziz, Adnan, Tsung-Hsien Lee, and Amit Prakash. *Elements of Programming Interviews: The Insider's Guide*. Seattle, WA: CreateSpace Independent Publishing Platform, 2012.
Aziz, Lee, and Prakash explore the types of problems candidates are given in job interviews for programming positions.

Connor, Joseph. *Programming: Computer Programming for Beginners: Learn the Basis of Java, SQL & C++*. Seattle, WA: CreateSpace Independent Publishing, 2015.
Connor discusses the basics of computer programming and covers the use of JavaScript, SQL, and C++.

Habgood, Jacob. *The Game Maker's Apprentice: Game Development for Beginners*. New York, NY: Apress, 2007.
Habgood guides the reader through the creation of nine video games using the video game creation tool Game Maker.

McDowell, Gayle Laakmann. *Cracking the Coding Interview: 189 Programming Questions and Solutions*. Palo Alto, CA: CareerCup Publishing, 2015.

McDowell discusses some of the more unique and difficult questions asked of programmers on job interviews and provides ways to think on your feet during an interview.

ORGANIZATIONS

Association of Information Technology Professionals
1120 Rout 73, Ste. 200
Mount Laurel, NJ 08054
(800) 224-9371
Website: http://www.aitp.org
AITP is an organization that advances the IT profession through support of education and professional development.

Women in Technology
200 Little Falls Street, Suite 205
Falls Church, VA 22046
(703) 349-1044
Women in Technology is an organization dedicated to the advancement of women in the technology industry.

JOURNALS

Edge
3 Queensbridge
The Lakes, Northampton NN4 7BF
England
+44 1604 251 045
Website: http://www.gamesradar.com/edge/
Edge offers news about the gaming industry for people
who work in the field or are interested in getting
involved in it. They provide features about how games
are made and coded and discuss the latest computer
programs for making games.

Gamasutra
303 2nd Street, 9th Floor
San Francisco, CA 94107
(415) 947-6000
Website: http://www.gamasutra.com
Gamasutra provides articles about the art and business
of making traditional games as well as video games
and mobile games.

WEBSITES

Due to the changing nature of internet links, Rosen Publishing has developed an online list of websites related to the subject of this book. This site is updated regularly. Please use this link to access the list:

http://www.rosenlinks.com/CCWC/game

CHAPTER 7

GET YOUR GAME DESIGN ON

Game design is a creative job in which one invents, creates, or assists in the creation of a game. In addition to the design of video games, a game designer can also design elements for tabletop games such as board games, card games, and role-playing games.

A video game designer tends to be a jack-of-all-trades and possesses working knowledge of all aspects of game creation, including programming, graphic design, art, writing, and managing. The lead game designer is usually the creative force behind a game's initial concept and often manages others who have more specific focused skills.

In larger teams, a game designer might work under a lead game designer and work on a more specific role in game creation. Smaller roles a game designer can have in a large team are:

- Level designer
- Writer and story development
- Artist and content design

Game designers need to have a general understanding of all areas of video game creation. They are responsible for bringing together the artist's vision for those who are coding, and are often the creators or major forces behind a game.

Specialized gaming camps are available to high school students and are a great place to learn valuable skills in all areas of the industry. They cover a varity of the skills that a game designer may need from concept to creation.

- Programmer
- System designer
- World designer
- Interface designer

Game designers can specialize in specific areas of game creation. Someone with a wide variety of gaming skills would do well as a game designer. In addition to the technical skills, a game designer must be able to see the overall big picture of the game creation process.

While programmers write detailed code, a game designer would have a general understanding of coding and be able to code to some extent. This would make the game designer a more effective communicator about how the game should be taking shape. Game designers direct the programmer and other team members. They communicate how to make adjustments, give creative criticisms, and handle schedules and deadlines. This means a game designer might also know how to design or draw. Seeing the big picture and knowing how to execute the project is the job of the game designer.

The job of a game designer or lead game designer is not an entry-level position. It requires experience with making games. The job does not necessarily require a college degree, however. The best way to show that you can master the job of a game designer is to do it by making a small-scale game yourself.

PREPARING YOURSELF

Inventing a game from scratch requires creativity, artistic skills, and programming all together. To become a game designer you should write and sketch out your ideas for video games. Familiarize yourself with programming, game engines, and the types of video games you wish to create. Drawing, art, graphic design, and programming are all courses or activities you should involve yourself with to become a game designer. Use online resources that are available. Try and create a simple video game and then move on to larger, more ambitious projects with friends.

FUTURE PROSPECTS

The US Bureau of Labor Statistics does not collect data on the video game industry or board game

Playing the latest video games is one of the many ways to immerse yourself in learning about the field. In additon to being good fun, it can be instructive to play different styles and types of games to understand how the elements combine.

FIFTEEN-YEAR-OLD GAME DESIGNER

Sometimes a simple idea is all that is required to become a video game designer and get noticed. An Australian teen named Ben Pasternak was only fourteen when he designed a game for his iPhone while he was in school. He used his laptop and some help from a programmer friend in Chicago, Austin Valleskey, to create the game *Impossible Rush* in just a few hours. The game became very popular in the Apple App Store and was downloaded five hundred thousand times in the first six weeks.

The success of *Impossible Rush* opened doors for Pasternak. He was invited to visit the offices of Google and Facebook. He visited Silicon Valley, California's technology center, in 2015 for a Google and MIT event called Hack Generation Y. The event draws applicants from high schools around the world. The 450 applicants who are accepted then create a game or app in thirty-six hours. Pasternak was one of just twenty students to be invited from outside the United States. In a 2015 interview with Mashable.com, Pasternak said he plans on "going to Apple's Worldwide Developers Conference, coming back to the U.S., and maybe getting an internship."

industry. However, the organization suggests that workers in this field earn more than the median annual income in the United States. The growing field is also an indication that future prospects in this area are strong.

FOR MORE INFORMATION

BOOKS

Brathwaite, Brenda, and Ian Schreiber. *Challenges for Game Designers.* Newton Centre, MA: Charles River Media, 2008.
Brathwaite and Schreiber present exercises that readers can follow to create their own game designs.

Rogers, Scott. *Level Up! The Guide to Great Video Game Design.* New York, NY: Wiley, 2014.
Rogers describes video game design, how to market your video game ideas, and how to create games for both mobile and console systems.

Schell, Jesse. *The Art of Game Design: A Book of Lenses.* Oxfordshire, England: AK Peters/CRC Press, 2014.
Schell, a top game designer, explains game design through the many "lenses" of people who view it from outside the field.

ORGANIZATIONS

Academy of Interactive Arts and Sciences (AIAS)
11175 Santa Monica Boulevard, 4th Floor
Los Angeles, CA 90025
(310) 484-2560

Website: http://www.interactive.org
The AIAS is a nonprofit organization dedicated to
  promoting the interactive arts, including video
  game arts.

Entertainment Software Association (ESA)
575 7th Street NW, Suite 300
Washington, DC 20004
Website: http://www.theesa.com
The ESA provides support for digital media
  professionals, including video game developers.

JOURNALS

International Journal of Computer Games Technology
315 Madison Avenue, 3rd Floor, Suite 3070
New York, NY 10017
Website: http://www.hindawi.com/journals/ijcgt
This journal publishes original research and review
  articles about games technology and interactive
  digital media.

WEBSITES

Due to the changing nature of internet links, Rosen Publishing has developed an online list of websites related to the subject of this book. This site is updated regularly. Please use this link to access the list:

http://www.rosenlinks.com/CCWC/game

CHAPTER 8

THE SOUND OF GAMING

Sound and music are sometimes overlooked as a career path in the video game industry. However, sound and music are just as important in games as they are in films. Many of the video games we love have iconic soundtracks and sound effects. Try and imagine classic games like *Pac-Man* or *Donkey Kong* without sound effects or a soundtrack. The experience would not be the same.

Today video games are more like motion pictures, with actors voicing game characters and famous composers creating game scores and directing orchestras. Video game music has become so popular that soundtracks are released alongside the

Video game sounds and music are an essential component in all video games. They help to create an environment and atmosphere for the game, as well as guiding gameplay. Above, a musician is recording a track in a studio.

video game. Sound design, music, and acting are all areas where jobs can be found in the game industry. Someone who loves video games and also loves music can combine the two seemingly incompatible skills in the gaming industry into a career path. Some of the jobs that may be available in the gaming industry include:

- Sound effects specialists
- Musicians
- Composers
- Conductors
- Voice actors
- Sound mixers
- Soundtrack developer
- Sound engineer

Each job involves a different level of expertise, from performing music to controlling computer software related to music. Many sound engineers have college degrees or even postgraduate degrees, but there are some jobs available at the assistant level that someone without a college degree can apply for.

Popular video games such as *Final Fantasy*, *The Legend of Zelda*, *Super Mario*, *Bioshock*, and *Silent Hill* all have soundtracks that were released digitally and on CD. Some video game soundtracks are even being released on vinyl. The soundtrack for the indie game *Fez* is available on the musician Disasterpeace's website digitally and

Musicians can find work in the video game industry by contributing to a game soundtrack or score. Mixing boards are used to combine a variety of tracks and recordings in a studio.

MAKING MONEY WITH MUSIC

Powerful music and sound creation apps can be purchased on mobile phones and tablets. These apps can be a good way to get started creating sounds and music for video games without having to invest in larger instruments.

Composers who retain the rights to their music can sell their game soundtracks online through websites like bandcamp.com. Selling your music online is a great way to make money. Soundcloud is another website for sharing music without allowing it to be downloaded. Meeting other musicians online and networking can help lead to freelance work and employment opportunities. People often look for new artists and sounds on these sites, and they provide good exposure for musicians who want to network with one another.

on vinyl. When a new video game is released, some have limited editions that contain extras such as art books and soundtracks that are not available elsewhere.

Music composition and creation has been steadily growing in the video game industry for many years. Many musicians and composers who have had a hard time finding work in the film industry have an easier time getting work for video games because of the sheer number of games being produced.

Almost all video games have music soundtracks and musicians can work on writing music, creating sound effects, or recording songs. Even a simple mobile app will require sound effects that can be created by someone who is musically inclined.

Voice-over acting and singing falls under the category of video game sound, too. Talented singers and actors are needed for these positions. Some celebrities have lent their acting and voice talents to video games, but that doesn't mean you need to be a famous actor to get a job in video game acting. Try answering ads for independent game developers making video games. They may have a need for voice talent but may not have a big budget. This is where you can build your résumé and get started working in the field.

PREPARING YOURSELF

Learning how to write music as well as mastering an instrument is important. Becoming versatile with different digital equipment such as electronic keyboards and music programs is also good preparation. Listen to sound effects and soundtracks for all kinds of video games. Even small games for mobile devices require sound effects and music. Create a digital sound effect library on your computer, and compose short instrumental pieces that can be used in a portfolio for your work.

Popular video game voice actor Troy Baker starred in *The Last of Us* and *Middle-earth: Shadow of Mordor*. Voice acting is an essential part of many video games. Many vioce actors work in a various of industries, of which video games is just one.

FUTURE PROSPECTS

According to the US Bureau of Labor Statistics, the job outlook for sound engineers is expected to grow in the next decade because of growth in multimedia products that offer audio and video capabilities. This includes video games in all platforms. Data is not collected for artists such as musicians and voice actors, but a similar growth can be expected.

WEBSITES

Due to the changing nature of internet links, Rosen Publishing has developed an online list of websites related to the subject of this book. This site is updated regularly. Please use this link to access the list:

http://www.rosenlinks.com/CCWC/game

CHAPTER 9

MAKE YOUR VIDEO GAME A REALITY

Do you have a great idea for a video game, but without financial resources or the backing of a large company? It may seem that there is little one can do to create something entirely alone. But there are options. If you or a small group of friends have the multiple well-rounded skills needed to create a game, then you might want to consider making it yourself. Many advanced video games like *Call of Duty* and *Assassin's Creed* require dozens or even hundreds of people to bring to completion. There have been some very fine examples of smaller, more intimate games created by individuals or small groups that have been successful.

Making a video game without the financial backing of a large company is not an easy undertaking, but it is by no means impossible. Today "indie" games, or independent video games made by a single person or small group without a video game publisher, are a growing force in the market.

Independent video game projects are being created, sold, and played all the time. Very large companies have

Virtual reality headsets are the next step in video games. Here, a gamer is wearing the popular "Oculus Rift" headset to play a game. This places the player in an immersive visual and auditory environment, making him or her feel that they are truly "in" the game.

even bought indie games after they received much success and praise in the market. One example is the virtual reality headset Oculus Rift. The headset displays video games in high definition. The project received its funding online at first and was then purchased by Facebook in 2014 for $2 billion. Development continued and the headset was released in 2016.

Indie games include games made for gaming consoles and also games for apps developed for Android or Apple phones. A college education is not required to make an indie game, but all of these features are needed if you want to be a successful entrepreneur in the video game industry:

- Hard work and dedication to the project
- Attention to the details required of a game designer or developer
- Knowledge of the video game industry and how to market and sell a game
- Knowledge of game design, programming, and graphic design
- Ability to deliver a product if financial backers are involved
- A basic understanding of how to finance, deliver, and market a product

Several documentary films have been made about the growing indie game phenomenon. One example is the 2012 film, *Indie Game: The Movie.* It features three popular video games: *Fez, Super Meat Boy,* and *Braid.* The movie chronicles the struggles and successes involved with indie game creation, development, and distribution. Phil Fish created the unique platform game *Fez,* which went on to win many gaming awards and is now sold on PlayStation, Xbox, and Steam. Edmund McMillen and Tommy Refenes created the platform game *Super Meat Boy* for Xbox, about a skinless boy searching for his girlfriend, who is made of bandages. The game went on to sell more than two million copies. And

Video game documentaries, such as *Indie Game: The Movie* are great resources for getting to know what the independent gaming industry is like.

Attending game developer conferences such as this one in San Francisco, California, is important for staying up-to-date on industry trends. Here, players and creators can interact, as well as present their ideas and projects to industry professionals and the media.

Jonathan Blow created *Braid*, which is one of the all-time highest-rated games.

GOING IT ALONE

A great way to stay involved in the gaming industry is to attend the annual Game Developers Conference (GDC) and the Independent Games Summit that is held there. This is the biggest annual gathering for gaming professionals. Attending the GDC is a great way to see what is being created, as well as a great opportunity to make connections in the gaming industry.

Another great resource for indie game developers is Steam, a website where many games, small and large, can get distributed for sale. While you may not get the in-store visibility that larger gaming companies have for their games, Steam has had sixty-five million users worldwide since 2014. Games on the website have a good chance of being seen and played.

INDIE SUCCESS STORIES

One of the biggest indie video game success stories of all time revolves around the popular building game *Minecraft*. Markus Persson, whose nickname is Notch, first created the game in which players build structures with cubes inside an open, virtual world. The game was created in 2009. The game's popularity took off and by 2014, Persson sold his company, Mojang, along with *Minecraft*, to Microsoft for $2.5 billion. As of 2015, over seventy million copies have been sold, making it one of the best-selling video games of all time.

Another indie success is the 2016 space exploration adventure game *No Man's Sky*, developed by the indie studio Hello Games. In the game, players can explore a vast universe with more than eighteen quintillion planets—more precisely, 18,446,744,073,709,551,616 of them! The development team grew from just four people to thirteen by the time the game was finished. That's not a lot of developers for a game so vast it would take a player five billion years to explore. It shows how much independent developers can accomplish.

PREPARING YOURSELF

Read trade publications and journals to keep informed about new platforms and game ideas. This can give you a head start brainstorming and creating content for what is to come. To create a video game independently you will need to stay focused on all aspects of game creation. In addition to the skills it takes to make and develop a game, you may want to take some business courses to help you through the process of funding and marketing your work.

FUTURE PROSPECTS

The US Bureau of Labor Statistics does not collect data about video game entrepreneurs, but has done studies about the work of established entrepreneurs in general. They have found that many get their start with entrepreneurialism as a second job. Some independent business ventures are successful, and some are not. The more prepared you are before taking financial risks, the better you will be in your business endeavors and future prospects. The area of independent game development is a growing field and will likely continue that way for many years.

FOR MORE INFORMATION

BOOKS

Diver, Mike. *Indie Games: The Complete Introduction to Indie Gaming.* Seattle, WA: Amazon Digital Services, 2016.
Diver provides an introduction to the indie gaming field, including insights on the differences between indie gaming companies and large commercial gaming companies.

Dreskin, Joel. *A Practical Guide to Indie Game Marketing.* Seattle, WA: Focal Press, 2015.
Dreskin gives practical advice about marketing an indie game on a limited budget and with limited resources and staff.

Hill-Whittall, Richard. *The Indie Game Developer Handbook.* Seattle, WA: Focal Press, 2015.
Hill-Whittall provides tips and advice for running an independent video game studio.

ORGANIZATIONS

National Association for the Self-Employed (NASE)
P.O. Box 241
Annapolis Junction, MD 20701-0241

(800) 649-6273
Website: http://www.nase.org
NASE provides guidance and resources for self-employed
people and small business owners.

National Small Business Association (NSBA)
P.O. Box 5024
Carefree, AZ 85377
(888) 800-3416
Website: http://www.nsba.net/contact-nsba
The NSBA is an organization dedicated to advocating
for small business owners to succeed on a state and
national level.

VIDEOS

"Game Loading: The Rise of the Indies" (http://www.
gameloading.tv)
This video discusses the subculture of independent game
development.

Indie Game: The Movie (http://buy.indiegamethemovie.com)
This film is a feature length documentary about the video
game industry.

Minecraft: The Story of Mojang (http://www.
minecraftstoryofmojang.com)
This film explores the rise of the independent video
game Minecraft.

WEBSITES

Due to the changing nature of internet links, Rosen
Publishing has developed an online list of websites
related to the subject of this book. This site is updated
regularly. Please use this link to access the list:

http://www.rosenlinks.com/CCWC/game

CHAPTER 10

MAKE YOUR HOBBY GAME A REALITY

Hobby games and family entertainment games have been a big business for generations. An entrepreneur can make a lot of money developing the next big game that people will want to play. Game companies such as Hasbro, Fantasy Flight Games, Paizo Inc., and Wizkids produce millions of dollars' worth of games each year. Sales from toy stores such as Toys "R" Us are in the billions. In 2014 alone, US sales revenues at Toys "R" Us reached $12.4 billion. A lot of this revenue comes from the sales of traditional board games, card games, and role-playing games.

Many people have good ideas for games, but bringing those ideas to life as a successful entrepreneur is another matter entirely. One of the most difficult challenges that young entrepreneurs face is coming up with the money to produce and distribute their game.

Traditional board and hobby games are also a large part of the gaming industry. Before video games, card and board games were major ways in which the public engaged in competive and shared gameplay. Some board games have ancient origins, and others are dependent on popular culture or clever mechanisms for engaging gameplay.

HAVING WHAT IT TAKES

Before you produce your game, you will need to take part in the following activities to be successful in your endeavor:

- Write a business plan that explains how many units you will produce, how much each will cost to make, and how much you will charge.
- Make a plan for distributing your goods locally, nationally, or globally.
- Create a plan to promote your product.
- Research funding your project, such as crowdsourcing or financial backers.
- Track all funds associated with the costs and profits of the business.
- Seek accounting help for the tax side of the business.
  Entrepreneurs must be ready to deal with unexpected problems with the business, so a good attitude and a personable outlook will go a long way when dealing with customers, financial backers, or business partners.

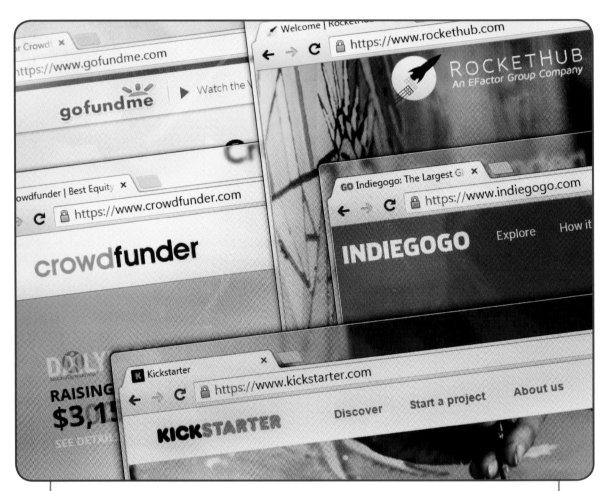

Crowdsourcing is a great way to raise funds to help make your video game a reality. Many projects that have trouble seeking tradtional investors take their funding into their own hands, bringing a crowdfunding campaign straight to the consumers who would be interested. The campaigns provide rewards and special discounts to those who buy into the project early to help secure funding.

CROWDSOURCING

Crowdsourcing is a popular way for independent game creators to obtain funding for a game project from a large group of people. People funding a crowdsourced project will often be compensated by being given the finished product when the project is complete. With this method, the financial backers can support a project they approve of or identify with, and the creator gets the money he or she needs to make a product.

The most popular crowdsourcing website is Kickstarter. com. One game created through crowdsourcing is the card game *Exploding Kittens*, which raised $8,782,571 on Kickstarter and became one of the most funded game campaigns of all time.

Be sure to check out other crowdsourcing websites such as indiegogo.com, crowdfunder.com, and rockethub.com, and follow the guidelines for creating crowd-sourced game projects for each site.

When getting funding for personal gaming projects proves too difficult, there are other options. For instance, board games and books for role-playing games need to be printed out, and this can be costly. To save on production costs and keep the selling price of your traditional game low, you can create a digital-only traditional board, card, or

THE INFLUENCE OF DUNGEONS AND DRAGONS

The most famous traditional indie game of all time, *Dungeons & Dragons*, is also known as D&D. Gary Gygax and Dave Arneson formed the company Tactical Studies Rules (TSR) in 1973 and first released their adventure game *Dungeons & Dragons* in 1974. The first D&D print run was just one thousand box sets that contained three game guides.

In the game, players create fictional characters on paper sheets and a single player, the Dungeon Master, (DM) describes the story adventure as well as the many characters, monsters, and environments the players encounter.

Dungeons & Dragons quickly became very popular and by 1981, TSR had revenues of $12.9 million. In 1997, the gaming company Wizards of the Coast purchased TSR for $25 million. The success of *Dungeons & Dragons* continued, and in 1999 the toy company Hasbro purchased Wizards of the Coast for $325 million.

The popularity of D&D went on to have a huge impact on video games and role-playing games alike. Video games from *Pokemon* to *Diablo* have all been influenced by Gygax and Arneson's home-brewed pen and paper game. Today D&D is in its fifth iteration.

RPG game. Then you can sell the digital files and have the gamer print out the game elements at home. Keep an open mind, stay creative, and do not get discouraged!

PREPARING YOURSELF

Being an entrepreneur of any kind starts with having a great idea that you think people will be interested in. Research traditional games and read periodicals about traditional games. These are great sources of inspiration. Also attend gaming conventions such as Gen Con. This annual gaming convention is a great place for game makers and game buyers to meet up, exchange ideas, and make some business deals.

FUTURE PROSPECTS

The future for any entrepreneur can be bright. Depending on your particular idea or project, the sky's the limit for what you can earn and the ideas you can develop. The more patience and determination you have, the greater your chances of success. This is not an endeavor, however, for someone who likes to play it safe and collect a steady paycheck.

FOR MORE INFORMATION

BOOKS

Boterman, Jack. *The Book of Games: Strategy, Tactics and History*. New York, NY: Sterling Publishing, 2008.
Boterman provides an overview of traditional gaming throughout history and its impact on games we play today.

Orbanes, Philip E. *The Game Makers: The Story of Parker Brothers, from Tiddley Winks to Trivial Pursuit*. Boston, MA: Harvard Business Review Press, 2003.
Orbanes gives an overview of the traditional game company, Parker Brothers, describing its challenges, successes, and climb to international fame over the course of the twentieth century and beyond.

Witwer, Michael. *Empire of Imagination: Gary Gygax and the Birth of Dungeons & Dragons*. New York, NY: Bloomsbury Publishing, 2015.
Witwer provides a history of independent game developer Gary Gygax and his role in the game industry.

ORGANIZATIONS

Entrepreneurs' Network
500 Montgomery Street, Suite 700
Alexandria, VA 22314
(703) 519-6700
Website: https://www.eonetwork.org
The Entrepreneurs' Network is a network of
    entrepreneurs from forty-eight countries, dedicated
    to networking with and helping other entrepreneurs.

Startup Grind
2555 Park Boulevard
Palo Alto, CA 94306
Website: https://www.startupgrind.com
Startup Grind is a start-up community meant to educate
    and inspire entrepreneurs and help them connect
    with one another.

WEBSITES

Due to the changing nature of internet links, Rosen Publishing has developed an online list of websites related to the subject of this book. This site is updated regularly. Please use this link to access the list:

http://www.rosenlinks.com/CCWC/game

GLOSSARY

CODE A program language for making computers follow a set of instructions.

COLOR THEORY The practice of mixing and combining colors in a pleasing way for artistic and communication practices.

COMPANY BRAND The marketing practice of creating a symbol or design that represents a company.

C++ LANGUAGE A computer programming language for writing object-oriented programming.

ENTREPRENEUR A person who organizes and operates a personal business.

ESPORTS Electronic sports; the industry of competitive, professional video gaming.

GAME DESIGN The process of designing a video game and its operations from the pre-production through production stages.

GAME ENGINE The basic software of a computer game or video game.

GRAPHIC DESIGN The job of combining text and pictures for a layout of a print or digital product.

HOBBY GAME Games played with dice, boards, cards, miniatures, tiles, and maps, such as *Dungeons & Dragons*; tabletop game.

INTERNSHIP A temporary position for a person who is new to a job field, either for no pay or for school credit.

JAVASCRIPT An object-oriented computer language used in programming.

LEAD DESIGNER A game designer who leads a team of other game designers with more focused specialties.

LICENSED PROPERTY A corporation-owned property that has been leased to another company to create goods based on it.

MOCKUP A model or arrangement meant to show what a real product will look like.

PROGRAMMING The process or action of writing programs for computers.

TABLETOP GAME Games played with dice, boards, cards, miniatures, tiles, and maps, such as *Dungeons & Dragons*; hobby game.

3-D ANIMATION Animating objects that appear in a three-dimensional space.

3-D RENDERING The process of converting 3-D wire frame models into 2-D images with 3-D photorealistic effects.

USER INTERFACE A device or program that allows a user to interact with a computer game or other multimedia source.

BIBLIOGRAPHY

Constine, Josh. "Facebook's $2 Billion Acquisition Of Oculus Closes, Now Official." Tech Crunch, July 21, 2014 (http://techcrunch.com/2014/07/21/facebooks-acquisition-of-oculus-closes-now-official/).

"Daily Report: Computer Technology Is Reviving the Board Game By The New York Times." *New York Times*, May 6, 2014 (http://bits.blogs.nytimes.com/2014/05/06/daily-report-computer-technology-is-reviving-the-board-game/).

Denhart, Chris. "How The $1.2 Trillion College Debt Crisis Is Crippling Students, Parents And The Economy." *Forbes*, August 7, 2013 (http://www.forbes.com/sites/specialfeatures/2013/08/07/how-the-college-debt-is-crippling-students-parents-and-the-economy/#10fcb8ae1a41).

Entis, Laura. "6 Tips From Kickstarter on How to Run a Successful Crowdfunding Campaign." Entreprenur, June 10, 2014 (http://www.entrepreneur.com/article/234707).

Francis, Hannah. "Is This 15-Year-Old Australian The Next Mark Zuckerberg?" SMH.com, October 8, 2014 (http://www.smh.com.au/digital-life/smartphone-apps/is-this-15yearold-australian-the-next-mark-zuckerberg-20141008-10rrzm.html).

Gaudiosi, John. "Mobile Game Revenues Set To Overtake Console Games in 2015." *Fortune*, January 15, 2015

(http://fortune.com/2015/01/15/mobile-console-game-revenues-2015).

Hamilton, Kirk. "Video Games are the New Best Way to Make a Living Composing Music." Kotaku, February, 23, 2012

(http://kotaku.com/5887745/video-games-are-the-new-best-way-to-make-a-living-composing-music).

"How to Become a Video Game Script Writer." A Digital Dreamer, March 23, 2016

(http://www.adigitaldreamer.com/articles/become-a-game-writer.htm).

Mac, Ryan. "Minecraft's Markus Persson Tells All On His Sale To Microsoft, His $70 Million Home And What's Next." *Forbes*, March 3, 2015

(http://www.forbes.com/sites/ryanmac/2015/03/03/minecraft-markus-persson-notch-interview-microsoft-sale/#69af39e410f3).

"Minecraft Reaches 70 Million Units Sold – Over 20 Million For PC." Legit Reviews, July 6, 2015 (http://www.legitreviews.com/minecraft-reaches-70-million-units-sold_167644).

Needleman, Sarah, E. "Inside the 'League of Legends' Championship at Madison Square Garden." *Wall Street Journal*, August 23, 2015 (http://blogs.wsj.com/digits/2015/08/23/e-sports-event-scores-at-madison-square-garden/).

Plumer, Brad. "Only 27 Percent Of College Grads Have A Job Related To Their Major." *Washington Post,* May 20, 2013 (https://www.washingtonpost.com/news/wonk/wp/2013/05/20/only-27-percent-of-college-grads-have-a-job-related-to-their-major/).

Ravitz, Jessica. "Varsity Gamers Making History And Dumbfounding Parents." CNN, Retrieved March 24, 2016 (http://www.cnn.com/interactive/2015/07/us/varsity-gamers-american-story/).

Refenes, Tommy. "How Do I Get Started Programming Games???" Gamasutra, January 7, 2013

(http://www.gamasutra.com/blogs/ TommyRefenes/20130107/184432/How_do_I_get_ started_programming_games.php).

Sinclair, Brendan. "Gaming Will Hit $91.5 Billion This Year—Newzoo." Giants Software, April 22, 2015

(http://www.gamesindustry.biz/articles/2015-04-22- gaming-will-hit-usd91-5-billion-this-year-newzoo).

Taylor, Ben. "Crowdfunding The Most Successful Kickstarter Campaigns of All Time." *Time*, April 8, 2015

(http://time.com/3770126/most-successful- kickstarter/).

"What is Game Design?" International Student, March 30, 2016

(http://www.internationalstudent.com/study-game- design/what-is-game-design/).

Wiltshire, Alex. "41 Amazing Things About No Man's Sky." Playstation, August 3, 2015

(http://blog.us.playstation.com/2015/08/03/35- amazing-things-about-no-mans-sky/).

"Work for Play: Careers in Video Game Development." Bureau of Labor Statistics, March 30, 2016 (http://www.bls.gov/careeroutlook/2011/fall/art01.pdf).

"Writing a Script for a Video Game." Storm the Castle, March 30, 2016 (http://www.stormthecastle.com/video-game-design/writing-a-video-game-script.htm).

INDEX

ABOUT THE AUTHOR

Adam Furgang was fortunate enough to be raised in the 1970s, the golden age of gaming. Among the first generation of kids to play video games at home, he has over three decades of experience playing video games, Dungeons & Dragons, and numerous other tabletop role-playing and board games. He continues to play games of all types with his two sons and runs a blog, *Wizards Never Wear Armor*, which covers gaming, art, and films.

PHOTO CREDITS

Cover, p. 3 John Williams Rus/Shutterstock.com; p. 6–7 M Bowles/Getty Images; pp. 10–11, 14–15, 116–117 Bloomberg/Getty Images; p. 13 © AP Images; pp. 22–23 Suzi Platt/FilmMagic/Getty Images; pp. 26–27 Imeh Akpanudosen/Getty Images; pp. 28–29 Diego Cervo/Shutterstock.com; pp. 30–31 Toshifumi Kitamura/AFP/Getty Images; pp. 36–37 Jupiterimages/Stockbyte/Thinkstock; pp. 40–41 Kaori Ando/Image Source/Getty Images; p. 45 Photofusion/Universal Images Group/Getty Images; pp. 50–51 Robyn Beck/AFP/Getty Images; pp. 52–53 Klaus Vedfelt/ Taxi/Getty Images; pp. 56–57 portishead1/E+/Getty Images; pp. 64–65 wavebreakmedia/ Shutterstock.com; pp. 66–67 © Bill Aron / PhotoEdit; pp. 68–69 JGI/Jamie Grill/Blend Images/Getty Images; pp. 78–79 Credit: Ariel Skelley/ Blend Images/Getty Images; pp. 80–81 © AP Images; pp. 82–82 Christian Science Monitor/Getty Images; pp. 90–91 Yuri Arcurs/Digital Vision/Getty Images; pp. 92–93 © aberCPC/Alamy Stock Photo; pp. 94–95 Hero Images/Getty Images; pp. 100–101 Terry Vine/Blend Images/Getty Images; p. 103 antb/Shutterstock.com; p. 106 Allen Berezovsky/Getty Images; pp. 112–113 Chesnot/Getty Images; p. 115 courtesy Everett Collection; pp. 124–125 © Valentino Visentini/Alamy Stock Photo; p. 126 © iStockphoto/GoodLifeStudio; interior pages graphic (controller icon) Bryan Solomon/Shutterstock.com.

Designer: Brian Garvey; Editor: Haley E. D. Houseman; Photo Researcher: Karen Huang